101 Bible Terms

Glen R. Landin

Copyright © 2016 Glen R. Landin.

No part of this publication may be reproduced or transmitted in any form or by any means, electronic or mechanical, including photocopying, recording, or by any information storage or retrieval system without written permission from the publisher.

Scriptures NIV are from The Holy Bible, New International Version®. © 1973, 1978, 1984 by International Bible Society. All rights reserved.

CREATIVEARTISTIC PUBLISHING
WWW.CREATIVEARTISTICPUBLISHING.COM
ORANGE, CALIFORNIA

ISBN -13 978-0996280747
ISBN -10 099628074X

PRINTED EDITION: APRIL 2016

PRINTED IN THE UNITED STATES OF AMERICA

WWW.GLENLANDIN.COM

GLEN R. LANDIN

The "101 Bible Terms" comprises some of
the most common and important words from The Holy
Bible. This book also includes a corresponding verse,
and a silhouette Bible on each page. All the selected
verses are taken from the NIV Bible. Perfect for Bible
studies, memorization, and personal spiritual
growth and reflection.

101 BIBLE TERMS

Amen

But grow in the grace and knowledge of our Lord and Savior Jesus Christ. To him be glory both now and forever! Amen

2 Peter 3:18 (NIV)

GLEN R. LANDIN

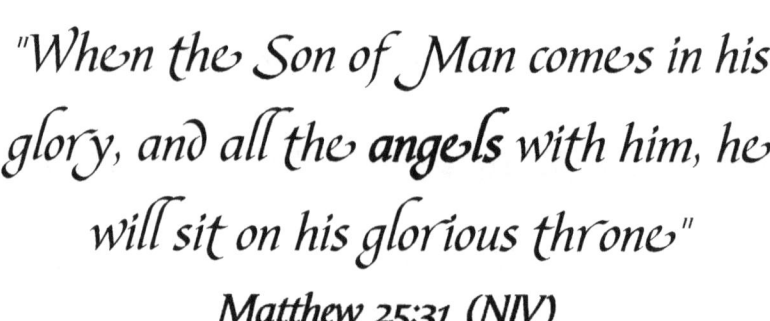

"When the Son of Man comes in his glory, and all the **angels** with him, he will sit on his glorious throne."
Matthew 25:31 (NIV)

101 BIBLE TERMS

Anoint

*Is anyone among you sick? Let them call the elders of the church to pray over them and **anoint** them with oil in the name of the Lord*
James 5:14 (NIV)

GLEN R. LANDIN

Apostle

*Paul, a servant of Christ Jesus, called to be an **apostle** and set apart for the gospel of God*
Romans 1:1 (NIV)

101 BIBLE TERMS

Ark

*When the **ark** of the LORD's covenant came into the camp, all Israel raised such a great shout that the ground shook*
1 Samuel 4:5 (NIV)

GLEN R. LANDIN

Atonement

*The rest of the oil in his palm the priest shall put on the head of the one to be cleansed and make **atonement** for them before the LORD*
Leviticus 14:18 (NIV)

101 BIBLE TERMS

Baptism

Before the coming of Jesus, John preached repentance and **baptism** *to all the people of Israel*
Acts 13:24 (NIV)

GLEN R. LANDIN

Bethany

When he had led them out to the vicinity of Bethany, he lifted up his hands and blessed them
Luke 24:50 (NIV)

101 BIBLE TERMS

Bethlehem

After Jesus was born in Bethlehem in Judea, during the time of King Herod, Magi from the east came to Jerusalem
Matthew 2:1 (NIV)

GLEN R. LANDIN

Birth

*Therefore, the Lord himself will give you a sign: The virgin will conceive and give **birth** to a son, and will call him Immanuel*

Isaiah 7:14 (NIV)

101 BIBLE TERMS

Blessing

*Praise be to the God and Father of our Lord Jesus Christ, who has blessed us in the heavenly realms with every spiritual **blessing** in Christ*

Ephesians 1:3 (NIV)

GLEN R. LANDIN

Census

*In those days Caesar Augustus issued a decree that a **census** should be taken of the entire Roman world*
Luke 2:1 (NIV)

101 BIBLE TERMS

Church

And I tell you that you are Peter, and on this rock I will build my **church**, *and the gates of death will not overcome it*
Matthew 16:18 (NIV)

GLEN R. LANDIN

Commandments

*These **commandments** that I give you today are to be on your hearts*
Deuteronomy 6:6 (NIV)

101 BIBLE TERMS

Cornerstone

*Built on the foundation of the apostles and prophets, with Christ Jesus himself as the chief **cornerstone***

Ephesians 2:20 (NIV)

GLEN R. LANDIN

Covenant

In the same way, after the supper he took the cup, saying, "This cup is the new **covenant** *in my blood, which is poured out for you"*
Luke 22:20 (NIV)

Creation

*Therefore, if anyone is in Christ, the new **creation** has come: The old has gone, the new is here!*
  2 Corinthians 5:17 (NIV)

GLEN R. LANDIN

Cross

Then Jesus said to his disciples, "Whoever wants to be my disciple must deny themselves and take up their cross and follow me."
Matthew 16:24 (NIV)

101 BIBLE TERMS

Crown of Thorns

*The soldiers twisted together a **crown of thorns** and put it on his head. They clothed him in a purple robe*
John 19:2 (NIV)

GLEN R. LANDIN

Crucified

"Therefore let all Israel be assured of this: God has made this Jesus, whom you **crucified**, both Lord and Messiah"
Acts 2:36 (NIV)

101 BIBLE TERMS

Dead Sea

*Its western border was the Jordan in the Arabah, from Kinnereth to the Sea of the Arabah (that is, the **Dead Sea**), below the slopes of Pisgah*
Deuteronomy 3:17 (NIV)

GLEN R. LANDIN

Disciple

Simon Peter and another disciple were following Jesus. Because this disciple was known to the high priest, he went with Jesus into the high priest's courtyard
John 18:15 (NIV)

101 BIBLE TERMS

Dissension

*A false witness who pours out lies and a person who stirs up **dissension** in the community*
Proverbs 6:19 (NIV)

GLEN R. LANDIN

Earth

Now the earth was formless and empty, darkness was over the surface of the deep, and the Spirit of God was hovering over the waters
Genesis 1:2 (NIV)

101 BIBLE TERMS

Edification

Let us therefore make every effort to do what leads to peace and to mutual edification

Romans 14:19 (NIV)

GLEN R. LANDIN

Emmanuel

*"The virgin will conceive and give birth to a son, and they will call him **Immanuel**" (which means "God with us")*
Matthew 1:23 (NIV)

101 BIBLE TERMS

Eternal Life

*For God so loved the world that he gave his one and only Son, that whoever believes in him shall not perish but have **eternal life***
John 3:16 (NIV)

GLEN R. LANDIN

Faith

*For it is by grace you have been saved, through **faith** - and this is not from yourselves, it is the gift of God*
Ephesians 2:8 (NIV)

101 BIBLE TERMS

Fellowship

*They devoted themselves to the apostles' teaching and to **fellowship**, to the breaking of bread and to prayer*
Acts 2:42 (NIV)

GLEN R. LANDIN

Fruit of the Spirit

But the fruit of the Spirit is love, joy, peace, patience, kindness, goodness, faithfulness
Galatians 5:22 (NIV)

101 BIBLE TERMS

Galilee

Now on his way to Jerusalem, Jesus traveled along the border between Samaria and Galilee
Luke 17:11 (NIV)

GLEN R. LANDIN

Garden of Eden

The LORD God took the man and put
him in the Garden of Eden to work it
and take care of it
Genesis 2:15 (NIV)

101 BIBLE TERMS

Gibeon

The king went to Gibeon to offer sacrifices, for that was the most important high place, and Solomon offered a thousand burnt offerings on that altar
1 Kings 3:4 (NIV)

GLEN R. LANDIN

In the beginning was the Word, and the Word was with God, and the Word was God
John 1:1 (NIV)

Gospel

He said to them, "Go into all the world and preach the **gospel** to all creation"
Mark 16:15 (NIV)

GLEN R. LANDIN

Hallelujah

*Then I heard what sounded like a great multitude, like the roar of rushing waters and like loud peals of thunder, shouting: "**Hallelujah!** For our Lord God Almighty reigns"*
Revelation 19:6 (NIV)

101 BIBLE TERMS

Heaven

Then I saw "a new **heaven** and a new earth," for the first **heaven** and the first earth had passed away, and there was no longer any sea
Revelation 21:1 (NIV)

GLEN R. LANDIN

Hell

For if God did not spare angels when they sinned, but sent them to hell, putting them in chains of darkness to be held for judgment
2 Peter 2:4 (NIV)

101 BIBLE TERMS

Holy

*But just as he who called you is **holy**, so be **holy** in all you do*
1 Peter 1:15 (NIV)

GLEN R. LANDIN

Holy Spirit

Therefore, go and make disciples of all nations, baptizing them in the name of the Father and of the Son and of the Holy Spirit
Matthew 28:19 (NIV)

101 BIBLE TERMS

Hope

*For I know the plans I have for you," declares the LORD, "plans to prosper you and not to harm you, plans to give you **hope** and a future*
Jeremiah 29:11 (NIV)

GLEN R. LANDIN

Hosanna

Those who went ahead and those who followed shouted, "Hosanna!" "Blessed is he who comes in the name of the Lord!"
Mark 11:9 (NIV)

101 BIBLE TERMS

Hymns

Speaking to one another with psalms, **hymns** and songs from the Spirit. Sing and make music from your heart to the Lord

Ephesians 5:19 (NIV)

GLEN R. LANDIN

Incense

*The high places, however, were not removed; the people continued to offer sacrifices and burn **incense** there*

2 Kings 12:3 (NIV)

101 BIBLE TERMS

Israel

"Therefore let all Israel be assured of this: God has made this Jesus, whom you crucified, both Lord and Messiah"
Acts 2:36 (NIV)

GLEN R. LANDIN

Jericho

These are the commands and regulations the LORD gave through Moses to the Israelites on the plains of Moab by the Jordan across from Jericho
Numbers 36:13 (NIV)

101 BIBLE TERMS

Jerusalem

On one occasion, while he was eating with them, he gave them this command: "Do not leave Jerusalem, but wait for the gift my Father promised, which you have heard me speak about"
Acts 1:4 (NIV)

GLEN R. LANDIN

Jesus

Jesus answered, "I am the way and the truth and the life. No one comes to the Father except through me"
John 14:6 (NIV)

101 BIBLE TERMS

Jordan

Jesus, full of the Holy Spirit, left the Jordan and was led by the Spirit into the wilderness
Luke 4:1 (NIV)

GLEN R. LANDIN

Jordan River

Confessing their sins, they were baptized by him in the Jordan River
Matthew 3:6 (NIV)

101 BIBLE TERMS

Consider it pure joy, my brothers and sisters, whenever you face trials of many kinds
James 1:2 (NIV)

GLEN R. LANDIN

Lord

If you declare with your mouth, "Jesus is Lord," and believe in your heart that God raised him from the dead, you will be saved

Romans 10:9 (NIV)

101 BIBLE TERMS

Love

*And we know that in all things God works for the good of those who **love** him, who have been called according to his purpose*
Romans 8:28 (NIV)

GLEN R. LANDIN

Manger

"This will be a sign to you: You will find a baby wrapped in cloths and lying in a manger"
Luke 2:12 (NIV)

101 BIBLE TERMS

Manna

The people of Israel called the bread **manna**. It was white like coriander seed and tasted like wafers made with honey
Exodus 16:31 (NIV)

GLEN R. LANDIN

Mediterranean Sea

"Your western boundary will be the coast of the Mediterranean Sea. This will be your boundary on the west"
Numbers 34:6 (NIV)

101 BIBLE TERMS

Message

Consequently, faith comes from hearing the **message**, and the **message** is heard through the word about Christ

Romans 10:17 (NIV)

GLEN R. LANDIN

Messenger

*This is the one about whom it is written: "I will send my **messenger** ahead of you, who will prepare your way before you"*
Luke 7:27 (NIV)

101 BIBLE TERMS

Minister

You learned it from Epaphras, our dear fellow servant, who is a faithful **minister** *of Christ on our behalf*
Colossians 1:7 (NIV)

GLEN R. LANDIN

Miracles

Remember the wonders he has done, his **miracles**, *and the judgments he pronounced*
Psalms 105:5 (NIV)

101 BIBLE TERMS

Mount of Olives

Jesus went out as usual to the Mount of Olives, and his disciples followed him
Luke 22:39 (NIV)

GLEN R. LANDIN

Nazareth

And he went and lived in a town called Nazareth. So was fulfilled what was said through the prophets: "He will be called a Nazarene."
Matthew 2:23 (NIV)

101 BIBLE TERMS

Offering

*"Speak to the Israelites and say to them: 'When you bring an **offering** to the LORD, bring as your **offering** an animal from either the herd or the flock"*

Leviticus 1:2 (NIV)

GLEN R. LANDIN

Parables

*Jesus spoke all these things to the crowd in **parables**; he did not say anything to them without using a parable*
Matthew 13:34 (NIV)

Passover

The disciples left, went into the city and found things just as Jesus had told them. So they prepared the Passover
Mark 14:16 (NIV)

GLEN R. LANDIN

Pastors

So Christ himself gave the apostles, the prophets, the evangelists, the pastors and teachers
Ephesians 4:11 (NIV)

101 BIBLE TERMS

Peace

*Therefore, since we have been justified through faith, we have **peace** with God through our Lord Jesus Christ*
Romans 5:1 (NIV)

GLEN R. LANDIN

Persecution

*Therefore, brothers and sisters, in all our distress and **persecution** we were encouraged about you because of your faith*

1 Thessalonians 3:7 (NIV)

101 BIBLE TERMS

Praise

Praise be to the God and Father of our Lord Jesus Christ, the Father of compassion and the God of all comfort
2 Corinthians 1:3 (NIV)

GLEN R. LANDIN

Prayer

*Do not be anxious about anything, but in every situation, by **prayer** and petition, with thanksgiving, present your requests to God*
Philippians 4:6 (NIV)

101 BIBLE TERMS

Promised Land

*By faith he made his home in the **promised land** like a stranger in a foreign country*
Hebrews 11:9 (NIV)

GLEN R. LANDIN

Prophecies

*Love never fails. But where there are **prophecies**, they will cease; where there are tongues, they will be stilled; where there is knowledge, it will pass away*
1 Corinthians 13:8 (NIV)

101 BIBLE TERMS

Prophet

"Before I formed you in the womb I knew you, before you were born I set you apart; I appointed you as a **prophet** to the nations"

Jeremiah 1:5 (NIV)

GLEN R. LANDIN

Red Sea

*So God led the people around by the desert road toward the **Red Sea**. The Israelites went up out of Egypt ready for battle*

Exodus 13:18 (NIV)

101 BIBLE TERMS

Redemption

*In him we have **redemption** through his blood, the forgiveness of sins, in accordance with the riches of God's grace*
Ephesians 1:7 (NIV)

GLEN R. LANDIN

Remembrance

And he took bread, gave thanks and broke it, and gave it to them, saying, "This is my body given for you; do this in remembrance of me."
Luke 22:19 (NIV)

101 BIBLE TERMS

Resurrection

Jesus said to her, "I am the resurrection and the life. Anyone who believes in me will live, even though they die"
John 11:25 (NIV)

GLEN R. LANDIN

Righteousness

But seek first his kingdom and his righteousness, and all these things will be given to you as well
Matthew 6:33 (NIV)

101 BIBLE TERMS

Risen

"Then go quickly and tell his disciples: 'He has **risen** from the dead and is going ahead of you into Galilee. There you will see him.' Now I have told you"

Matthew 28:7 (NIV)

GLEN R. LANDIN

Even though I walk through the darkest valley, I will fear no evil, for you are with me; your rod and your staff, they comfort me
Psalms 23:4 (NIV)

101 BIBLE TERMS

Sabbath

"Remember the Sabbath day by keeping it holy"
Exodus 20:8 (NIV)

GLEN R. LANDIN

Sacrifices

This is why he has to offer **sacrifices** for his own sins, as well as for the sins of the people
Hebrews 5:3 (NIV)

101 BIBLE TERMS

Salvation

"**Salvation** is found in no one else, for there is no other name given under heaven by which we must be saved"
Acts 4:12 (NIV)

GLEN R. LANDIN

Savior

*While we wait for the blessed hope - the appearing of the glory of our great God and **Savior**, Jesus Christ*
Titus 2:13 (NIV)

101 BIBLE TERMS

Scripture

*All **Scripture** is God-breathed and is useful for teaching, rebuking, correcting and training in righteousness*
2 Timothy 3:16 (NIV)

GLEN R. LANDIN

Scrolls

When you come, bring the cloak that I left with Carpus at Troas, and my scrolls, especially the parchments
2 Timothy 4:13 (NIV)

101 BIBLE TERMS

Sea of Galilee

*Some time after this, Jesus crossed to the far shore of the **Sea of Galilee** (that is, the Sea of Tiberias)*
John 6:1 (NIV)

GLEN R. LANDIN

Seals

Then I saw in the right hand of him who sat on the throne a scroll with writing on both sides and sealed with seven seals
Revelation 5:1 (NIV)

101 BIBLE TERMS

Serpent

He seized the dragon, that ancient **serpent**, who is the devil, or Satan, and bound him for a thousand years

Revelation 20:2 (NIV)

GLEN R. LANDIN

Sinner

*He replied, "Whether he is a **sinner** or not, I don't know. One thing I do know. I was blind but now I see!"*
John 9:25 (NIV)

101 BIBLE TERMS

Spear

*Instead, one of the soldiers pierced Jesus' side with a **spear**, bringing a sudden flow of blood and water*
John 19:34 (NIV)

GLEN R. LANDIN

Staff

*Even though I walk through the darkest valley, I will fear no evil, for you are with me; your rod and your **staff**, they comfort me*
Psalms 23:4 (NIV)

101 BIBLE TERMS

Stone Tablets

*At the end of the forty days and forty nights, the LORD gave me the two **stone tablets**, the tablets of the covenant*

Deuteronomy 9:11 (NIV)

GLEN R. LANDIN

Tabernacle

*In the same way, he sprinkled with the blood both the **tabernacle** and everything used in its ceremonies*
Hebrews 9:21 (NIV)

101 BIBLE TERMS

Temple

Jesus answered them, "Destroy this temple, and I will raise it again in three days"
John 2:19 (NIV)

GLEN R. LANDIN

Testimony

And this gospel of the kingdom will be preached in the whole world as a **testimony** to all nations, and then the end will come

Matthew 24:14 (NIV)

101 BIBLE TERMS

Tithe

"A **tithe** of everything from the land, whether grain from the soil or fruit from the trees, belongs to the LORD; it is holy to the LORD"

Leviticus 27:30 (NIV)

GLEN R. LANDIN

Tomb

*Finally the other disciple, who had reached the **tomb** first, also went inside. He saw and believed*
John 20:8 (NIV)

101 BIBLE TERMS

Unleavened Bread

*Although the priests of the high places did not serve at the altar of the LORD in Jerusalem, they ate **unleavened bread** with their fellow priests*
2 Kings 23:9 (NIV)

GLEN R. LANDIN

Witness

*He came as a **witness** to testify concerning that light, so that through him all might believe*
John 1:7 (NIV)

101 BIBLE TERMS

Worship

Therefore, I urge you, brothers and sisters, in view of God's mercy, to offer your bodies as a living sacrifice, holy and pleasing to God - this is true **worship**

Romans 12:1 (NIV)

GLEN R. LANDIN

About The Author

Glen Landin continues writing unique and informative books. In this release entitled, "101 Bible Terms", he combines the most common words from the Bible which includes a corresponding verse, and a silhouette Bible.

As a creative writer and author, Glen also enjoys interior design, photography, model railroading, visual displays, and traveling to nearby and distant shores.

Through Glen's creative writing skills, using poems, phrases, affirmations, and messages, he inspires, encourages, and motivates people to simply believe in yourself. Because all things are possible to those who believe!